BAD

PERIL

AN

ABIAN

ALE

STORY BY
MARIE P. CROALL
PENCILS AND INKS BY
CLINT HILINSKI

OTTOMAN
EMPIRE
(TURKEY)

N

MEDITERRANEAN

SEA

THE
MIDDLE EAST

THIS MAP SHOWS THE MIDDLE EAST AS IT WAS
KNOWN AROUND A.D. 1500, WHEN THE SINBAD
STORIES WERE COLLECTED AND WRITTEN IN ARABIC.

SINBAD
SAILING INTO PERIL

AN
ARABIAN
TALE

BAGHDAD

P E R S I A
(I R A N)

M E S O P O T A M I A
(I R A Q)

Tigris River

Euphrates River

BASSORAH
(BASRA)

CARLETON PLACE
PUBLIC LIBRARY

A R A B I A
(S A U D I A R A B I A)

GRAPHIC UNIVERSE™ • MINNEAPOLIS

Sinbad is a character in *Arabian Nights*, a classic work of Arabian literature. Also known as *The Thousand and One Nights*, the book is made up of approximately 200 tales from Persia, India, and other nations in and near the Middle East. The *Arabian Nights* stories were collected and written down in Arabic around a.d. 1500. In the 1880s, British scholars Sir Richard F. Burton and John Payne translated the stories into English. Featuring enchanting characters and amazing story lines, the tales have captured readers' imaginations for generations.

In adapting the story of Sinbad, author Marie P. Croall worked from *Arabian Nights Volume I: The Marvels and Wonders of the Thousand and One Nights*, adapted from Richard F. Burton's unexpurgated translation by Jack Zipes. Artist Clint Hilinski consulted numerous historical resources and collaborated with Allan T. Kohl, an art historian and visual resources librarian at the Minneapolis College of Art and Design. Kohl has studied the *Arabian Nights* tales and authored an article on *Sinbad* for *Medieval Trade, Travel, and Exploration: An Encyclopedia*.

STORY BY MARIE P. CROALL

PENCILS AND INKS BY CLINT HILINSKI

COLORING BY HI–FI DESIGN

LETTERING BY BILL HAUSER

CONSULTANT: ALLAN T. KOHL, M.A.,
MINNEAPOLIS COLLEGE OF ART AND DESIGN

Graphic Universe™
A division of Lerner Publishing Group, Inc.
241 First Avenue North
Minneapolis, MN 55401 U.S.A.

Website address: www.lernerbooks.com

Library of Congress Cataloging-in-Publication Data

Croall, Marie P.
    Sinbad : sailing into Peril / by Marie P. Croall ; pencils and inks by Clint Hilinski.
      p.   cm. — (Graphic myths and legends)
    "Adapted from Arabian Nights Volume I: The Marvels and Wonders of the Thousand and One Nights."
    Summary: Recounts, in comic book format, Sinbad's adventurous sea voyages that made him wealthy and famous.
    ISBN-13: 978-0-8225-6375-4 (lib. bdg. : alk. paper)
    ISBN-10: 0-8225-6375-4 (lib. bdg. : alk. paper)
    1. Sinbad (Legendary character)—Legends—Comic books, strips, etc. [1. Sinbad (Legendary character)—Legends. 2. Fairy tales. 3. Arabs—Folklore. 4. Folklore—Arab countries. 5. Cartoons and comics.] I. Hilinski, Clint, ill. II. Sindbad the sailor. III. Arabian nights. IV. Title. V. Series.
PZ8.C8684Si 2008
741.5'973—dc22   2006003968

Manufactured in the United States of America
2 3 4 5 6 7 – DP – 13 12 11 10 09 08

TABLE OF CONTENTS

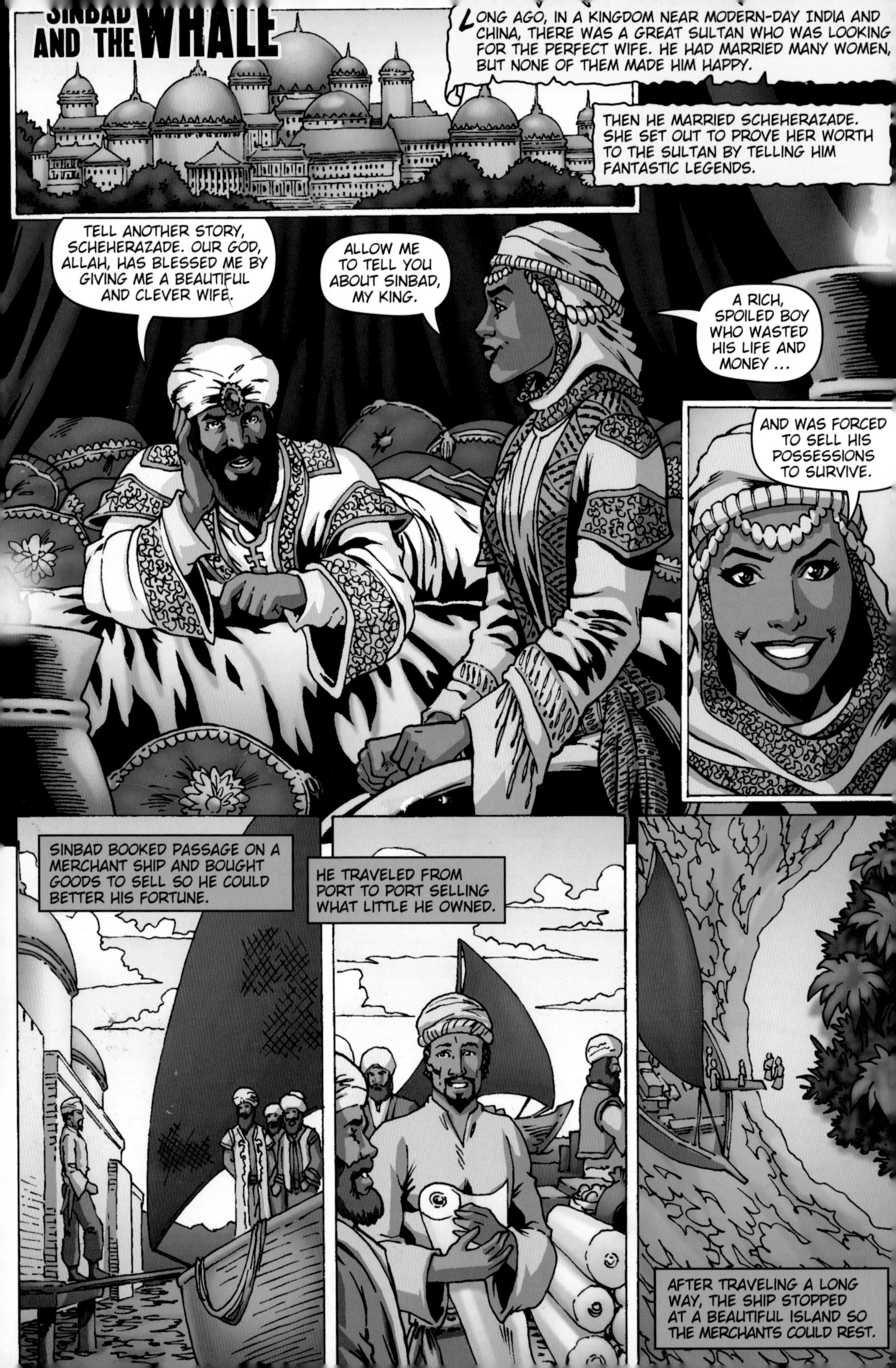
SINBAD AND THE WHALE
LONG AGO, IN A KINGDOM NEAR MODERN-DAY INDIA AND CHINA, THERE WAS A GREAT SULTAN WHO WAS LOOKING FOR THE PERFECT WIFE. HE HAD MARRIED MANY WOMEN, BUT NONE OF THEM MADE HIM HAPPY.
THEN HE MARRIED SCHEHERAZADE. SHE SET OUT TO PROVE HER WORTH TO THE SULTAN BY TELLING HIM FANTASTIC LEGENDS.
TELL ANOTHER STORY, SCHEHERAZADE. OUR GOD, ALLAH, HAS BLESSED ME BY GIVING ME A BEAUTIFUL AND CLEVER WIFE.
ALLOW ME TO TELL YOU ABOUT SINBAD, MY KING.
A RICH, SPOILED BOY WHO WASTED HIS LIFE AND MONEY ...
AND WAS FORCED TO SELL HIS POSSESSIONS TO SURVIVE.
SINBAD BOOKED PASSAGE ON A MERCHANT SHIP AND BOUGHT GOODS TO SELL SO HE COULD BETTER HIS FORTUNE.
HE TRAVELED FROM PORT TO PORT SELLING WHAT LITTLE HE OWNED.
AFTER TRAVELING A LONG WAY, THE SHIP STOPPED AT A BEAUTIFUL ISLAND SO THE MERCHANTS COULD REST.

THE MEN SET UP A PLACE TO SLEEP BEFORE THEY WENT TO EXPLORE THE ISLAND.

THAT EVENING SINBAD WAS RELAXING BY THE FIRE WHEN SUDDENLY ...

RUN FOR YOUR LIVES!

RETURN TO THE SHIP, AND SAVE YOURSELVES!

MAY ALLAH PRESERVE YOU. THIS ISLAND IS NOT AN ISLAND BUT A HUGE WHALE!

WHEN YOU LIT A FIRE, IT FELT THE HEAT AND MOVED.

IT WILL DIVE UNDERWATER IN A MOMENT, AND WE WILL BE DROWNED!

SINBAD RAN AS FAST AS HE COULD TO GET TO THE SHIP.

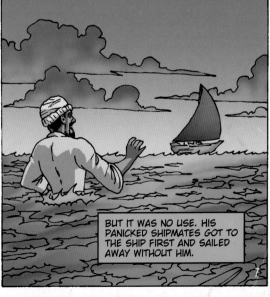

BUT IT WAS NO USE. HIS PANICKED SHIPMATES GOT TO THE SHIP FIRST AND SAILED AWAY WITHOUT HIM.

7

SINBAD STRUGGLED TERRIBLY IN THE OCEAN WATERS—UNTIL HE SPOTTED A WOODEN TUB FLOATING BY.

GASP! CHOKE!

PRAISE ALLAH!

SINBAD TRAVELED FOR DAYS IN THE TUB BEFORE PASSING OUT FROM HUNGER AND EXHAUSTION.

FINALLY, HE LANDED ON A BEACH.

HE WAS FAR FROM CIVILIZATION, SO SINBAD WAS SURPRISED TO SEE A HORSE THERE.

WHERE COULD THIS HORSE HAVE COME FROM?

SINBAD APPROACHED THE HORSE CAREFULLY, WHEN SUDDENLY A MAN APPEARED.

YOU THERE! WHAT ARE YOU DOING HERE?

MY SHIP SAILED AWAY, AND I WASHED ASHORE.

I MEAN YOU NO HARM AND SEEK ONLY FOOD AND WATER.

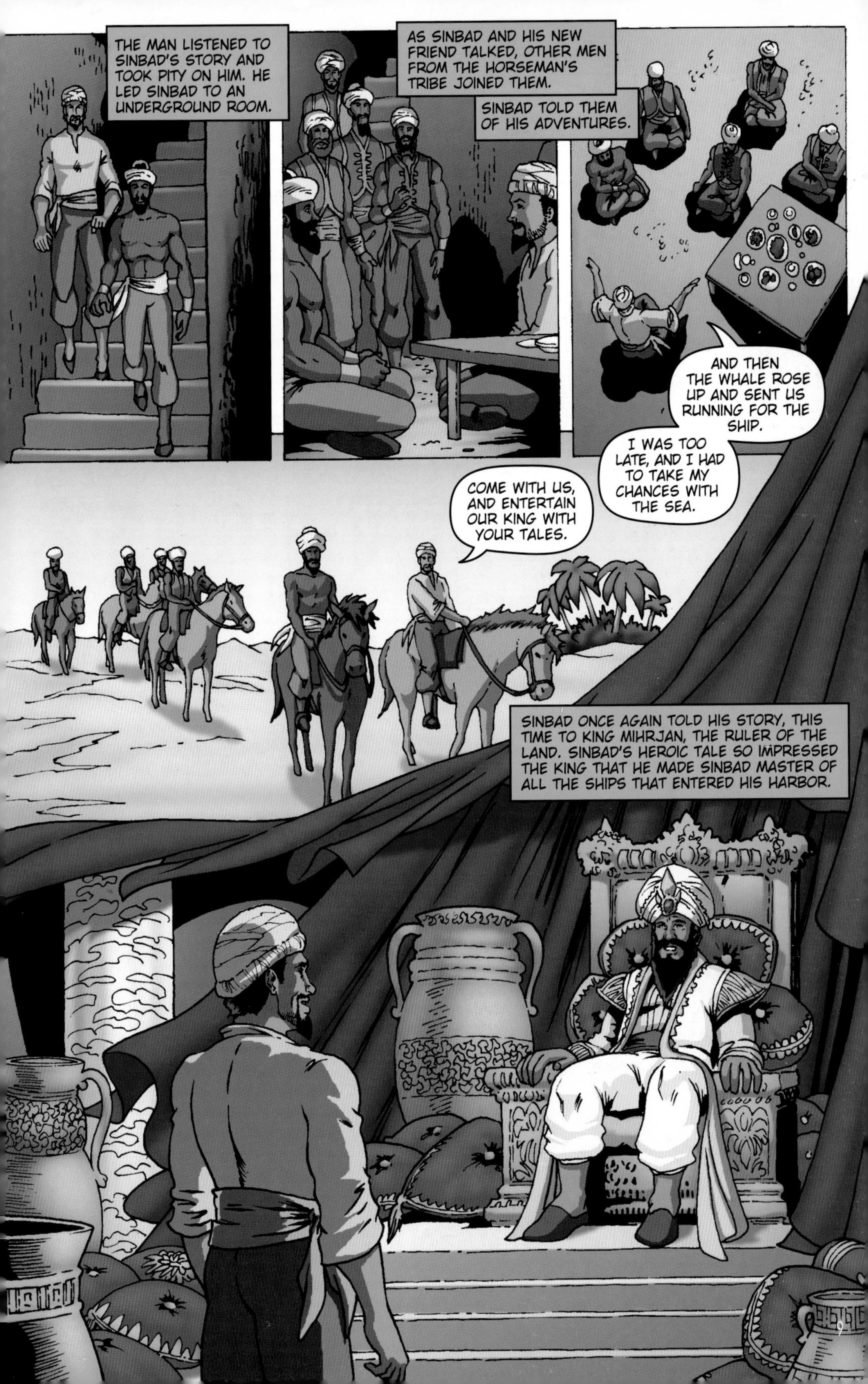
THE MAN LISTENED TO SINBAD'S STORY AND TOOK PITY ON HIM. HE LED SINBAD TO AN UNDERGROUND ROOM.
AS SINBAD AND HIS NEW FRIEND TALKED, OTHER MEN FROM THE HORSEMAN'S TRIBE JOINED THEM.
SINBAD TOLD THEM OF HIS ADVENTURES.
AND THEN THE WHALE ROSE UP AND SENT US RUNNING FOR THE SHIP.
I WAS TOO LATE, AND I HAD TO TAKE MY CHANCES WITH THE SEA.
COME WITH US, AND ENTERTAIN OUR KING WITH YOUR TALES.
SINBAD ONCE AGAIN TOLD HIS STORY, THIS TIME TO KING MIHRJAN, THE RULER OF THE LAND. SINBAD'S HEROIC TALE SO IMPRESSED THE KING THAT HE MADE SINBAD MASTER OF ALL THE SHIPS THAT ENTERED HIS HARBOR.

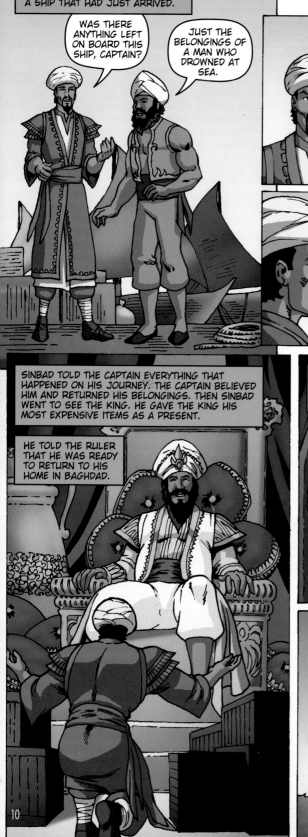

WAS THERE ANYTHING LEFT ON BOARD THIS SHIP, CAPTAIN?

JUST THE BELONGINGS OF A MAN WHO DROWNED AT SEA.

WHAT WAS THIS MAN'S NAME?

WE CALLED HIM *SINBAD*.

I AM SINBAD!

HOW CAN I BE SURE?

SINBAD TOLD THE CAPTAIN EVERYTHING THAT HAPPENED ON HIS JOURNEY. THE CAPTAIN BELIEVED HIM AND RETURNED HIS BELONGINGS. THEN SINBAD WENT TO SEE THE KING. HE GAVE THE KING HIS MOST EXPENSIVE ITEMS AS A PRESENT.

HE TOLD THE RULER THAT HE WAS READY TO RETURN TO HIS HOME IN BAGHDAD.

IN RETURN, THE KING'S MEN PRESENTED SINBAD WITH A GIFT AND WISHED HIM WELL ON HIS JOURNEY.

SINBAD HEADED FOR HOME, ANXIOUS TO RETURN TO THE LAND HE LOVED.

SINBAD AND THE RUKH

ARE YOU READY FOR ANOTHER TALE, HUSBAND?

CERTAINLY, MY DEAR WIFE. TELL ME WHAT HAPPENS TO SINBAD NEXT.

BEFORE TOO LONG, SINBAD GREW TIRED OF LIFE AT HOME AND STRUCK OUT ON ANOTHER JOURNEY.

THE SHIP ANCHORED SO THE MEN COULD EXPLORE A NEWLY DISCOVERED ISLAND.

AFTER WALKING AROUND THE ISLAND FOR A WHILE, SINBAD GREW SLEEPY AND STOPPED TO TAKE A QUICK NAP.

BUT WHEN HE AWOKE, HE FOUND THAT THE SHIP HAD LEFT WITHOUT HIM.

HE WAS DESERTED ON THE STRANGE ISLAND.

SINBAD EXPLORED THE REST OF THE ISLAND AND FOUND SOMETHING STRANGE.

AFTER EXAMINING THE OBJECT CAREFULLY, HE RECOGNIZED IT AS A RUKH'S EGG, HAVING HEARD STORIES ABOUT THE HUGE BIRDS.

PRAISE ALLAH ...

LOOKING AT THE RUKH, SINBAD CAME UP WITH A WAY TO GET OFF THE ISLAND.

AFTER USING HIS TURBAN TO TIE HIMSELF TO THE BIRD, SINBAD WAS CARRIED AWAY.

THE RUKH DROPPED SINBAD ON A ROCKY CLIFF.

SINBAD NOTICED DIAMONDS ON THE GROUND. HE WAS SURPRISED TO FIND GEMS IN THIS LOCATION.

ALLAH, BE WITH ME.

I AM IN A WORSE PLACE THAN THE ONE I JUST LEFT.

SINBAD CONTINUED EXPLORING HIS SURROUNDINGS. THERE WERE SOME BEAUTIFUL GEMS IN THE AREA, BUT IT WAS NOT A SAFE PLACE.

THUMP!

SINBAD EXAMINED THE JEWEL-STUDDED MEAT.

HE HAD HEARD OF THIS WAY OF COLLECTING GEMS, BUT HE HAD NEVER SEEN IT BEFORE.

MEN WOULD THROW THE MEAT, AND THE GEMS WOULD STICK TO IT. THEN BIRDS WOULD CARRY THE MEAT BACK TO THE MEN SO THEY COULD COLLECT THE TREASURES.

SINBAD USED HIS TURBAN TO TIE HIMSELF TO THE MEAT ...

AND PRAYED THE BIRDS WOULD CARRY HIM TO A SAFER PLACE.

CAW!! CAW!!

SINBAD'S PLAN WORKED. BUT WHEN THE BIRD DROPPED SINBAD, HIS ARRIVAL STARTLED A MAN WHO'D BEEN COLLECTING GEMS.

AAAHHHHH!!

BROTHER, I MEAN NO HARM. I AM A GOOD MAN AND A MERCHANT.

I HAVE LOTS OF DIAMONDS FOR YOU, BETTER THAN YOU WOULD OTHERWISE GET.

HOW DID YOU COME TO BE HERE?

SINBAD GAVE THE MAN SOME OF THE BIGGEST DIAMONDS AND TOLD HIM HIS STORY.

AND I HOPED TYING MYSELF TO THE MEAT WOULD LEAD ME TO SAFETY.

YOU MUST STAY WITH US IN MY VILLAGE UNTIL YOU CAN RETURN TO YOUR BELOVED BAGHDAD.

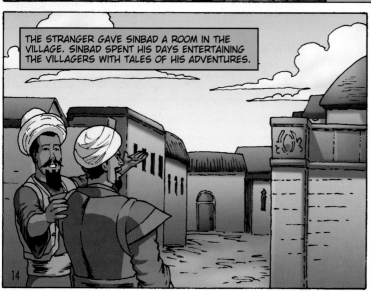

THE STRANGER GAVE SINBAD A ROOM IN THE VILLAGE. SINBAD SPENT HIS DAYS ENTERTAINING THE VILLAGERS WITH TALES OF HIS ADVENTURES.

14

WHEN SINBAD RETURNED TO BAGHDAD, HE WON GREAT RICHES AND HONORS FOR HIS ADVENTURES.

SINBAD AND THE OGRE

BUT SINBAD WAS READY FOR MORE ADVENTURE. HE SOON PLANNED ANOTHER TRIP.

WE'VE SAILED OFF COURSE AND ARE TOO NEAR THE MOUNTAIN OF THE ZUGHB.

NO MAN HAS EVER COME AWAY FROM THERE ALIVE.

NO SOONER HAD THE CAPTAIN SPOKEN THAN *APES* LEAPED ONTO THE BOAT.

ALLAH, SAVE US!

THE APES TOOK CONTROL OF THE SHIP AND LEFT SINBAD AND HIS MEN ON THE MOUNTAIN.

THE MEN HAD TO EXPLORE THE ISLAND. THEY WERE HUNGRY AND HAD TO FIND FOOD.

RIGHT BEFORE DARK, THEY FOUND A LARGE CASTLE.

15

THEY WENT INTO THE CASTLE HOPING TO FIND SHELTER.

WHAT KIND OF MONSTER WOULD USE SUCH A LARGE COOKING POT?

I DON'T THINK WE'RE SAFE HERE.

THE EXHAUSTED MEN HAD NO CHOICE BUT TO SLEEP IN THE CASTLE. SINBAD AND ANOTHER MAN KEPT WATCH.

BEFORE LONG, AN EVIL CREATURE APPEARED.

AN OGRE! ALLAH, SAVE US!

THE MEN WATCHED IN HORROR AS THE OGRE TOOK THE CAPTAIN.

THE MEN KNEW THEY HAD TO FIND A WAY OFF THE ISLAND.

IT DIDN'T TAKE SINBAD LONG TO COME UP WITH A PLAN.

IT IS BETTER WE FIGHT THAN WAIT FOR THE OGRE TO RETURN.

I SAY WE TAKE OUR CHANCES TO ESCAPE.

SOME OF THE MEN GATHERED WOOD FROM THE ISLAND AND MADE A SIMPLE RAFT.

THE OTHERS READIED THE WEAPONS THEY FOUND IN THE CASTLE.

THE NEXT TIME THE OGRE SHOWED UP, THE MEN ATTACKED.

THEY USED THE SKEWERS IN THE COOKING POT TO BLIND THE MONSTER.

ARRRRGGH!!

RUN!!

17

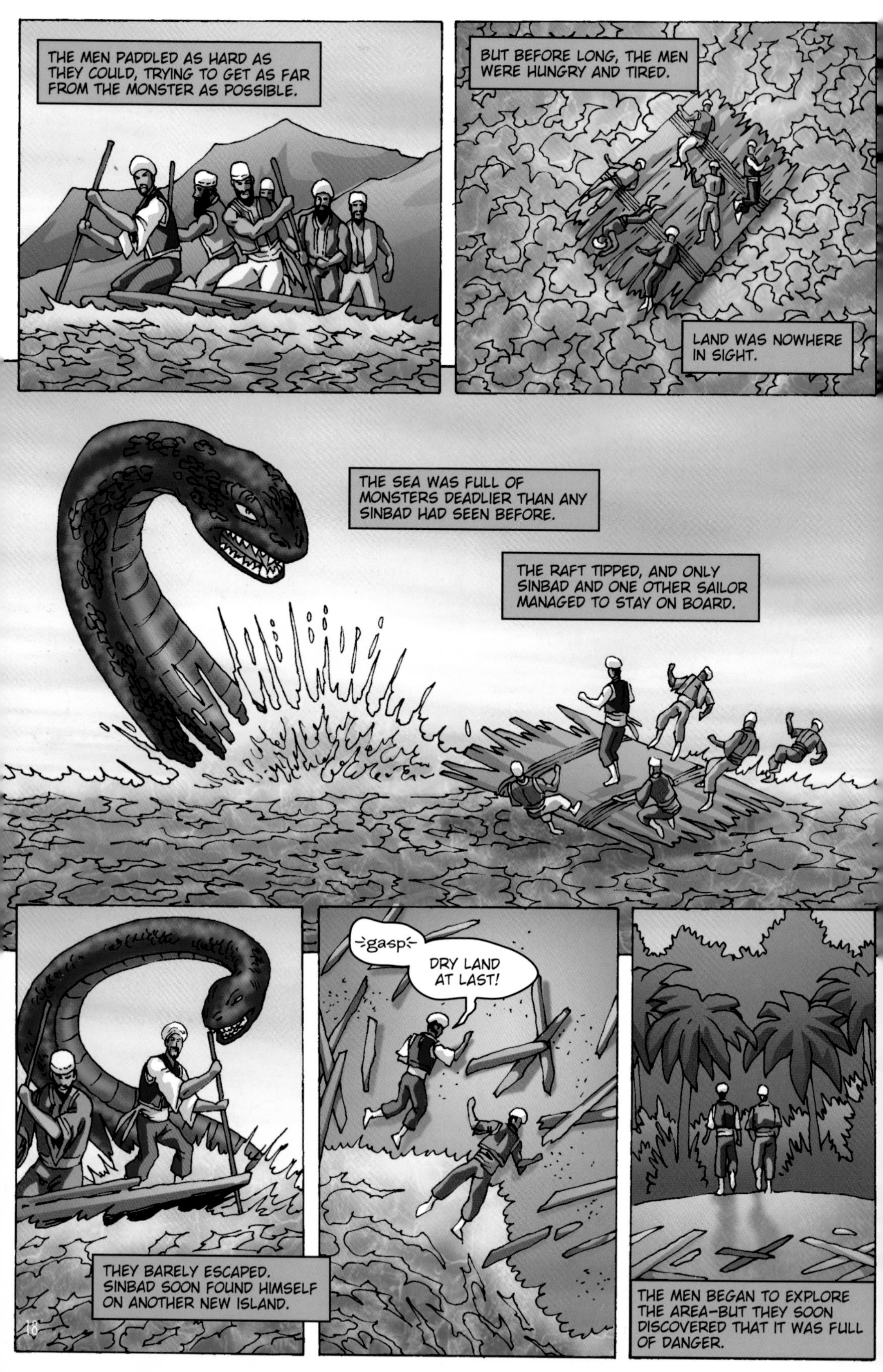

THE MEN PADDLED AS HARD AS THEY COULD, TRYING TO GET AS FAR FROM THE MONSTER AS POSSIBLE.
BUT BEFORE LONG, THE MEN WERE HUNGRY AND TIRED.
LAND WAS NOWHERE IN SIGHT.
THE SEA WAS FULL OF MONSTERS DEADLIER THAN ANY SINBAD HAD SEEN BEFORE.
THE RAFT TIPPED, AND ONLY SINBAD AND ONE OTHER SAILOR MANAGED TO STAY ON BOARD.
THEY BARELY ESCAPED. SINBAD SOON FOUND HIMSELF ON ANOTHER NEW ISLAND.
gasp
DRY LAND AT LAST!
THE MEN BEGAN TO EXPLORE THE AREA—BUT THEY SOON DISCOVERED THAT IT WAS FULL OF DANGER.

DO YOU FEEL LIKE WE'RE BEING WATCHED?

WE'RE NOT SAFE HERE. CAN WE KEEP MOVING?

THEY FOUND A SPOT TO REST FOR THE NIGHT. BUT THE ISLAND'S SNAKE LURKED JUST ABOVE THEM IN A TREE.

IN THE MORNING, SINBAD FOUND THAT THE SNAKE HAD TAKEN HIS FRIEND.

HE'S GONE!

SINBAD SAW THE SNAKE WATCHING HIM, AND HE KNEW THAT IT WOULD COME FOR HIM THAT NIGHT.

SSSSSSSSSSSSSSSSSSSSSS!!

HE QUICKLY THOUGHT OF THE PERFECT PLAN.

THAT NIGHT SINBAD WAITED FOR THE SNAKE TO RETURN.

THAT BIG SNAKE CAN'T SWALLOW THESE LOGS.

SINBAD WAS SAFE FROM THE SNAKE THAT NIGHT, BUT HE KNEW HE HAD TO GET OFF THE ISLAND.

HE TRIED TO ESCAPE.

BUT THERE WAS NOWHERE TO GO. SOON HE WAS NEAR DEATH FROM HUNGER.

JUST WHEN HE THOUGHT HE WAS FINISHED ...

PRAISE ALLAH! A SHIP! I AM RESCUED!

HELP! OVER HERE!

THE MERCHANTS ON THE SHIP WERE ONLY TOO HAPPY TO RESCUE HIM AND BRING HIM BACK TO BAGHDAD.

AT HOME SINBAD TOLD HIS STORY TO HIS AWESTRUCK FRIENDS.

BUT HE KNEW HE HAD NOT YET TAKEN HIS LAST JOURNEY.

SINBAD AND THE OLD MAN

ONCE AGAIN, SINBAD ARRANGED PASSAGE ON A SHIP. HE WAS READY FOR ANOTHER ADVENTURE.

AND ONCE AGAIN, THE TRIP WAS FULL OF DANGER.

WHAT COULD IT BE?

I'VE NEVER SEEN ANYTHING LIKE IT.

IF WE BREAK IT, WE COULD FIND GOLD AND RICHES INSIDE!

STOP! THE BIRDS WILL COME AND KILL US!

21

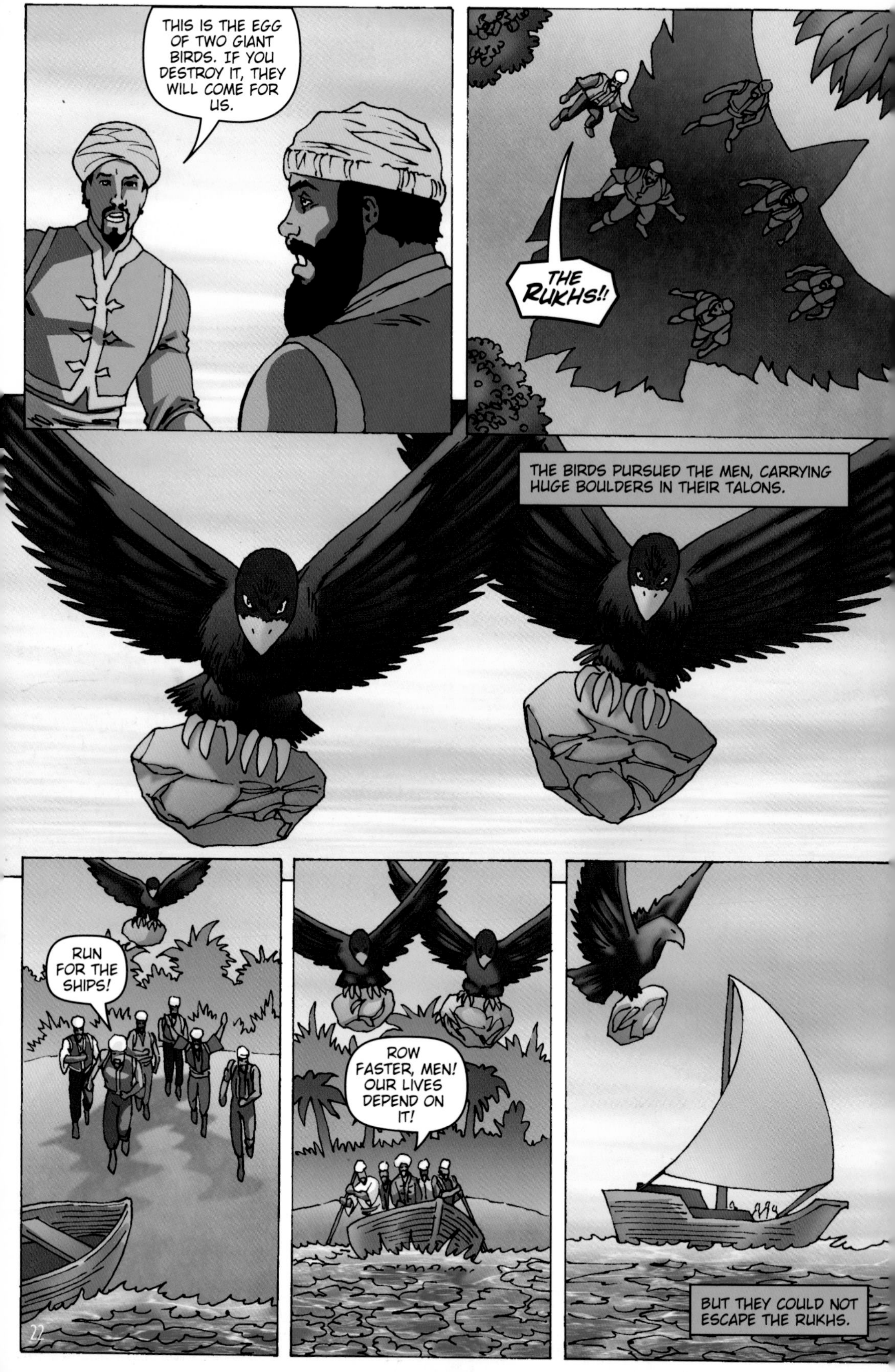
THIS IS THE EGG OF TWO GIANT BIRDS. IF YOU DESTROY IT, THEY WILL COME FOR US.
THE RUKHS!!
THE BIRDS PURSUED THE MEN, CARRYING HUGE BOULDERS IN THEIR TALONS.
RUN FOR THE SHIPS!
ROW FASTER, MEN! OUR LIVES DEPEND ON IT!
BUT THEY COULD NOT ESCAPE THE RUKHS.

THE RUKHS HAVE TOPPLED OUR SHIP!

WE'RE GOING UNDER!

I MUST SWIM TO SAFETY!

SINBAD REACHED AN ISLAND JUST AS HIS STRENGTH WAS ABOUT TO GIVE OUT.

HE KNEW HE WAS FAR FROM HOME AND HAD NO WAY OFF THE ISLAND.

SINBAD LIVED ON THE FRUIT THAT GREW ON THE ISLAND.

AND THE ISLAND WAS SAFE, SO SINBAD COULD SLEEP WITHOUT WORRY.

AFTER A FULL NIGHT'S SLEEP, SINBAD SET OUT TO EXPLORE HIS TEMPORARY HOME.

24

SOON SINBAD CAME UPON AN OLD MAN BY THE RIVERBANK.

SIR, DO YOU NEED ANY HELP?

THE MAN POINTED URGENTLY TO THE OTHER SIDE OF THE RIVER.

I CAN CARRY YOU ACROSS THE RIVER.

CLIMB UP, FRIEND.

SINBAD WAS HAPPY TO HELP THE OLD STRANGER CROSS THE RIVER.

SINBAD TRIED TO MAKE CONVERSATION.

SIR, WHAT BRINGS YOU TO THIS FAR-OFF LAND?

BUT HE GOT NO RESPONSE.

SIR ...?

FINALLY, THEY REACHED THE OTHER SIDE OF THE RIVER.

WE'VE CROSSED THE RIVER. YOU CAN GET DOWN NOW.

THE MAN REFUSED TO GET OFF SINBAD'S SHOULDERS.

OW! ALL RIGHT, I'LL KEEP WALKING!

HE TIGHTENED HIS LEGS WHEN HE WANTED SINBAD TO WALK FASTER. THE OLD MAN WAS SURPRISINGLY STRONG, AND SINBAD COULD NOT FREE HIMSELF FROM HIS VIOLENT HOLD.

26

SINBAD WALKED ON THROUGH THE NIGHT, WAITING FOR A WAY TO GET RID OF THE MAN.

HE SAW SOME BERRIES NEARBY AND CAME UP WITH AN IDEA.

SINBAD SQUEEZED JUICE FROM THE BERRIES INTO A HOLLOW GOURD.

THEN HE WAITED FOR THE JUICE TO FERMENT.

WHEN THE TIME WAS RIGHT, HE PULLED OUT THE GOURD.

I SURE COULD USE A NIIIICE ... COOOOL ... DRINK!

SINBAD HELD THE GOURD SO THE MAN WOULD SEE IT. HE KNEW FERMENTED JUICE WOULD MAKE THE MAN WOOZY.

JUST AS SINBAD HAD PLANNED, THE MAN GRABBED THE GOURD.

ENJOY!

GLUG!

GLUG!!

GLUG!!

SOON THE OLD MAN WAS WOOZY FROM THE JUICE.

AND NOT TOO LONG AFTER THAT, HE WAS UNCONSCIOUS.

SLEEP WELL, SIR!

SINBAD CAREFULLY PUT THE SLEEPING MAN ON THE GROUND.

THEN HE RAN AS FAR AWAY FROM THE MAN AS HE COULD.

HE STOPPED WHEN THE MAN WAS NO LONGER IN SIGHT.

BY THAT TIME, HE WAS ON THE BEACH AT THE OTHER SIDE OF THE ISLAND.

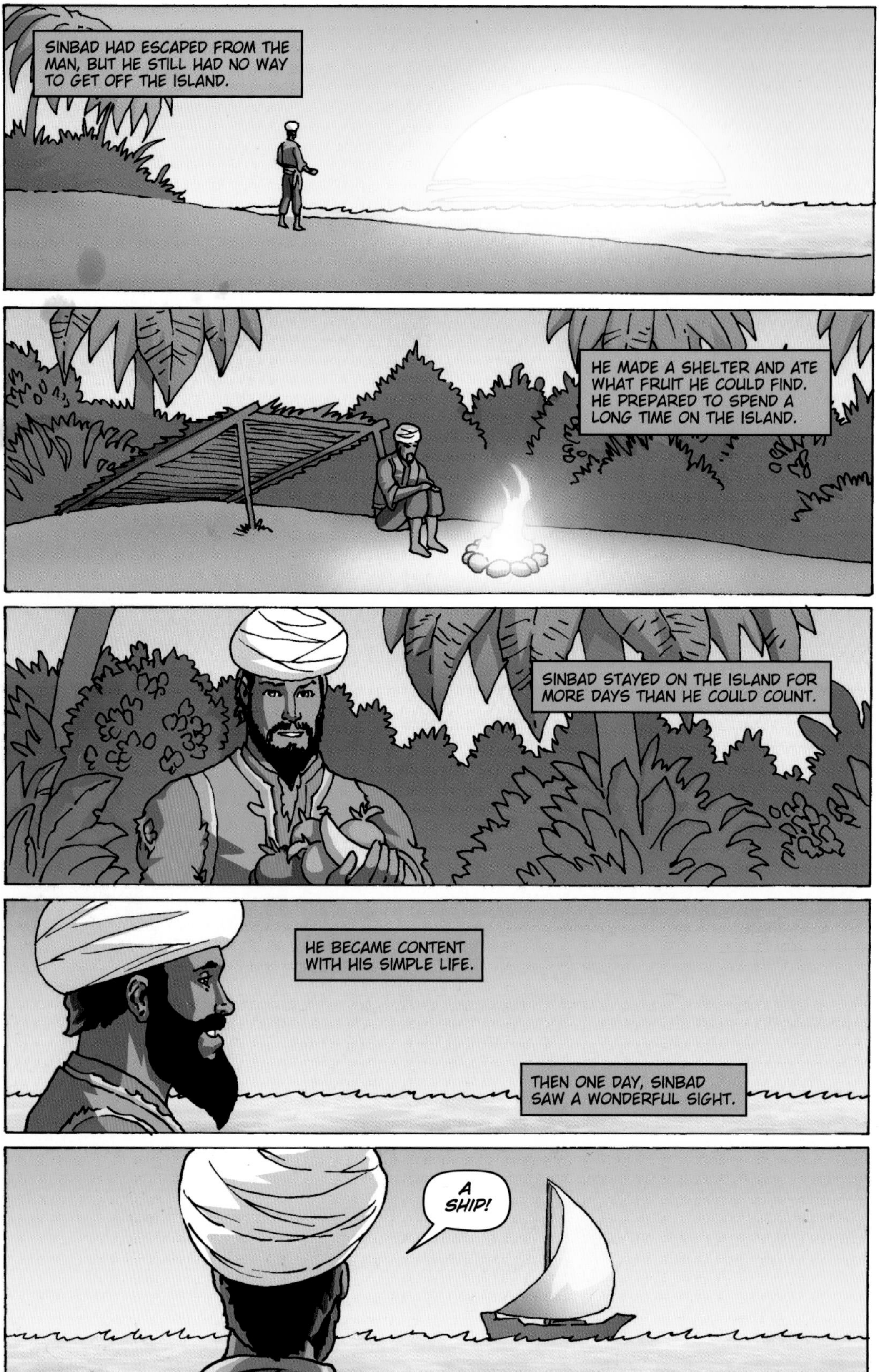

SINBAD HAD ESCAPED FROM THE MAN, BUT HE STILL HAD NO WAY TO GET OFF THE ISLAND.
HE MADE A SHELTER AND ATE WHAT FRUIT HE COULD FIND. HE PREPARED TO SPEND A LONG TIME ON THE ISLAND.
SINBAD STAYED ON THE ISLAND FOR MORE DAYS THAN HE COULD COUNT.
HE BECAME CONTENT WITH HIS SIMPLE LIFE.
THEN ONE DAY, SINBAD SAW A WONDERFUL SIGHT.
A SHIP!

THE MEN ON THE SHIP SAW SINBAD'S FIRE AND CAME TO SEE WHO LIVED ON THE ISLAND.

AHOY, FRIEND! TELL US HOW YOU CAME TO BE HERE.

AND THAT'S WHEN I BUILT THE SHELTER. I'VE BEEN LIVING HERE EVER SINCE.

WE CAN TAKE YOU BACK TO OUR HOME. YOU CAN STAY THERE UNTIL YOU FIND A WAY TO BAGHDAD.

SINBAD SAILED OFF WITH THE MEN, HAPPY TO HAVE FOUND REAL FOOD AND FRIENDSHIP.

RESCUED AT LAST!

SOON THE SHIP LANDED IN A STRANGE LOCATION.

THIS IS THE CITY OF THE APES. WE CAN'T BE HERE AT NIGHT.

THAT'S WHEN THE APES ATTACK.

OOOOOHEEE!

BEWARE THOSE BEASTS!

THE STRANGE SIGHTS IN THE CITY MADE SINBAD LONG FOR HOME. HE TOLD HIS COMPANIONS OF HIS HOMESICKNESS.

SO YOU NEED MONEY TO PAY FOR YOUR TRIP TO BAGHDAD?

YES, I LOST MY POSSESSIONS WHEN MY SHIP WAS WRECKED.

I THINK I CAN HELP YOU.

SINBAD SOON BEGAN GATHERING ROCKS FROM THE GROUND, JUST AS HIS NEW FRIEND HAD TOLD HIM TO DO.

THESE APES ARE THE TICKET BACK TO MY HOMELAND.

WITH THE ROCKS IN HAND, SINBAD APPROACHED THE APES.

TAKE THAT!

AND THAT!!

THE APES THREW COCONUTS AT SINBAD IN RETALIATION. IT WAS JUST WHAT SINBAD HAD HOPED THEY WOULD DO. HE GATHERED THE FRUITS.

COCONUTS FOR SALE!

GET SOME SWEET, DELICIOUS COCONUT FRUITS!

SINBAD SOLD ENOUGH COCONUTS TO PAY FOR HIS TRIP HOME.

AHH! HOME AT LAST!

AND HE WAS CONTENT THERE, FOR A WHILE.

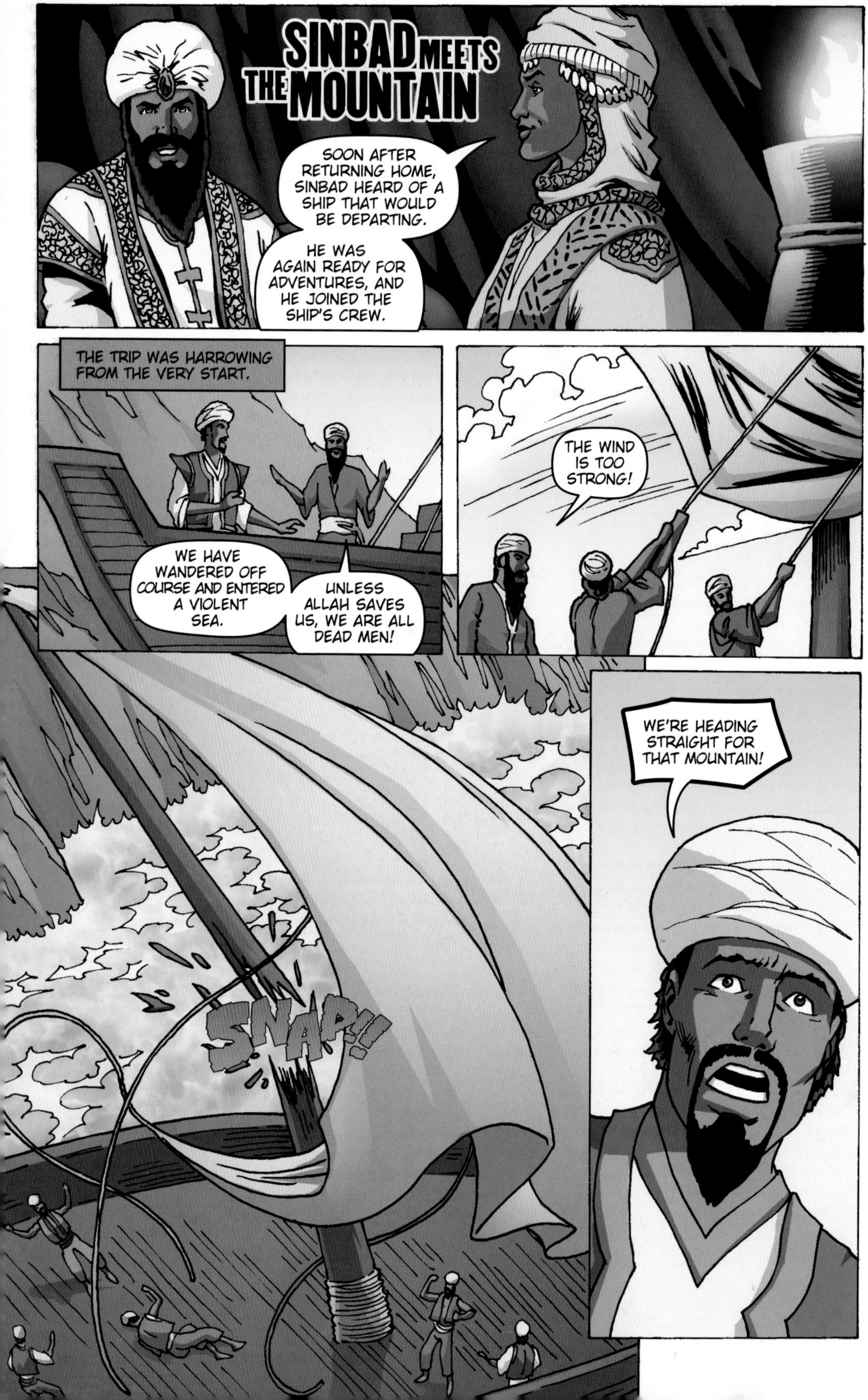

SINBAD MEETS THE MOUNTAIN
SOON AFTER RETURNING HOME, SINBAD HEARD OF A SHIP THAT WOULD BE DEPARTING.
HE WAS AGAIN READY FOR ADVENTURES, AND HE JOINED THE SHIP'S CREW.
THE TRIP WAS HARROWING FROM THE VERY START.
WE HAVE WANDERED OFF COURSE AND ENTERED A VIOLENT SEA.
UNLESS ALLAH SAVES US, WE ARE ALL DEAD MEN!
THE WIND IS TOO STRONG!
SNAP!!
WE'RE HEADING STRAIGHT FOR THAT MOUNTAIN!

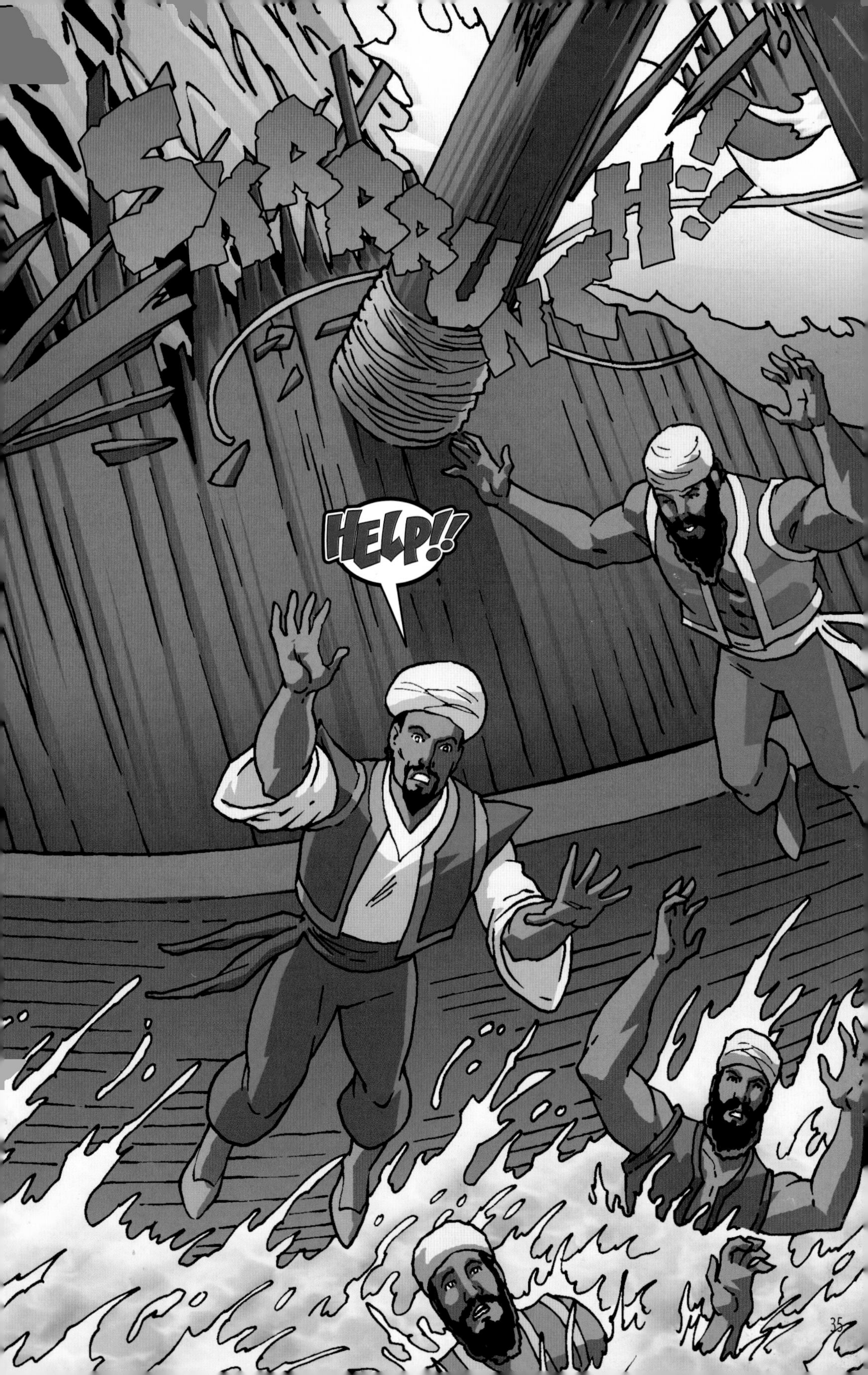

SKRRUNCH!!
HELP!!

THE SHIP BROKE INTO PIECES WHEN IT CRASHED INTO THE MOUNTAIN. BUT SINBAD LIVED THROUGH THE WRECK—AND SO DID THE OTHER MEN ON THE SHIP.

COME, MEN, WE WILL FIND REST ON THE OTHER SIDE OF THIS MOUNTAIN.

A SURPRISE GREETED THE MEN WHEN THEY REACHED THE MOUNTAIN'S TOP.

I'VE NEVER SEEN SUCH RICHES!

WHEN WE RETURN HOME, WE WILL BE WEALTHY MEN. GATHER WHAT FOOD AND GEMS YOU CAN.

THE MEN ALSO FOUND FRUIT-BEARING TREES ON THE MOUNTAIN.

BUT ALL TOO SOON THEY DISCOVERED THAT THE FRUIT WAS NOT FIT TO EAT.

I FEAR MY MEN WILL NOT MAKE IT THROUGH THE NIGHT.

THE FRUIT ... IT MUST HAVE GONE BAD.

SOON SINBAD WAS ALONE ON THE ISLAND. HIS MEN HAD DIED AFTER EATING THE BAD FRUIT. SINBAD CONTINUED TO EXPLORE ON HIS OWN.

SINBAD REMEMBERED THE RAFT HE'D BUILT BEFORE TO ESCAPE THE OGRE AND DECIDED TO MAKE ANOTHER ONE.

BUT THE RIVER QUICKLY BECAME ROUGH AND DANGEROUS.

SINBAD FLOATED INTO A CAVE SO SMALL THAT HE COULD BARELY RAISE HIS HEAD.

GET ME OUT OF THIS DARK TUNNEL!

EACH BEND OF THE RIVER BROUGHT A NEW SURPRISE.

BEFORE LONG, SINBAD FOUND HIMSELF IN A VILLAGE. HE WAS BOTH EXCITED AND SCARED WHEN HE SAW THE VILLAGERS.

A STRANGER HAS WASHED UP ON OUR SHORE!

THE VILLAGERS TOOK SINBAD TO SEE THEIR KING.

I COME FROM THE LAND RULED BY THE GREAT CALIPH HARUN AL-RASHID, A FAIR AND JUST KING.

STAY WITH ME, SINBAD, AND TELL ME ABOUT THE LAWS OF YOUR CALIPH, SO I TOO CAN BE A GREAT RULER.

SINBAD LIVED IN HONOR WITH THE KING. HE TAUGHT THE RULER ALL ABOUT THE LAWS OF CALIPH HARUN AL-RASHID.

TELL ME MORE!

BUT SINBAD WOULDN'T STAY WITH THE KING FOR LONG.

AS HE WAS WALKING OUTSIDE THE KING'S PALACE ONE DAY, SINBAD WAS SHOWN A SIGHT THAT PLEASED HIM GREATLY.

SINBAD! THERE IS A SHIP THAT CAN RETURN YOU TO YOUR HOMELAND!

WE WILL MISS YOU, SINBAD. MAY ALLAH BE WITH YOU.

SINBAD THANKED THE KING FOR HIS HOSPITALITY AND PREPARED FOR A HASTY DEPARTURE.

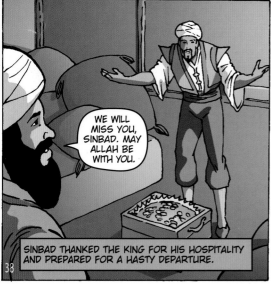

WHEN HE RETURNED HOME, SINBAD SHARED HIS STORIES WITH HIS CALIPH, WHO GAVE HIM MANY GIFTS AND HONORS.

SINBAD AND THE DEMONS

SINBAD'S LAST VOYAGE WOULD BE HIS MOST AMAZING.

TIRED OF HIS LIFE AT HOME, SINBAD WENT TO BASSORAH, WHERE HE FOUND A SHIP READY TO SAIL.

BUT THE WEATHER WAS BAD AND THE WIND TOO STRONG FOR THE SHIP.

ALLAH, SAVE US! WINDS HAVE BLOWN US TO AN OCEAN FILLED WITH DEADLY CREATURES.

HERE COMES ONE NOW!

A WHALE UPSET THE SHIP, TILTING IT BACKWARD VIOLENTLY.

THE WHALE MOVED IN FRONT OF THE SHIP, READY TO SWALLOW IT WHOLE.

AS THE MEN PRAYED FOR HELP, A FIERCE STORM PULLED THE SHIP FROM THE WHALE.

THE STORM TOSSED THE SHIP INTO A ROCKY REEF.

TERRIFIED, SINBAD MADE A PROMISE.

IF ALLAH SAVES ME, I WILL NEVER AGAIN TRAVEL ON THE HIGH SEAS!

I WILL NEVER AGAIN SUFFER FOR MY GREED.

I WILL BUILD ANOTHER RAFT, AND IF I AM SAVED, IT WILL BE BY ALLAH'S GRACE.

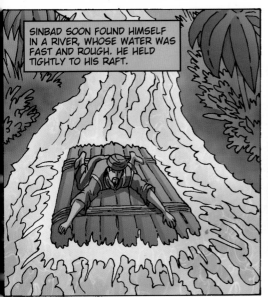

SINBAD SOON FOUND HIMSELF IN A RIVER, WHOSE WATER WAS FAST AND ROUGH. HE HELD TIGHTLY TO HIS RAFT.

ALLAH, SAVE ME!

AAAAAHHHH!

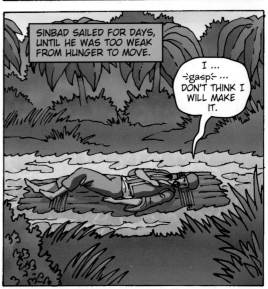

SINBAD SAILED FOR DAYS, UNTIL HE WAS TOO WEAK FROM HUNGER TO MOVE.

I ... ≈gasp≈ ... DON'T THINK I WILL MAKE IT.

AFTER A WHILE, THE RIVER CARRIED SINBAD INTO A VILLAGE.

THE VILLAGERS QUICKLY CAME TO HIS AID AND TOOK SINBAD TO THEIR RULING SHEIKH.

THE SHEIKH GAVE SINBAD MANY DELICIOUS AND NOURISHING FOODS. SOON HIS HEALTH WAS RESTORED.

IF YOU HADN'T FOUND ME, I DON'T KNOW WHAT I WOULD HAVE DONE.

PLEASE, STAY HERE IN THE VILLAGE WITH US.

I HAVE A HOUSE YOU CAN STAY IN WHILE YOU ARE HERE.

SEVERAL DAYS LATER, THE SHEIKH CAME TO SEE SINBAD.

I'LL BUY YOUR GOODS FOR A FAIR PRICE.

WHAT GOODS?

THE WOOD FROM YOUR RAFT.

I TRUST YOU. I'LL ACCEPT YOUR OFFER.

THE SHEIKH HAD ANOTHER OFFER THAT WAS EVEN BETTER.

I HAVE FOUND THE PERFECT BRIDE FOR YOU, IF YOU WILL HAVE HER.

I TRUST YOU, SHEIKH. I WILL MARRY HER.

SO SINBAD MARRIED. HIS BRIDE WAS BEAUTIFUL AND KIND, AND SHE AND SINBAD LOVED EACH OTHER VERY MUCH.

AFTER LIVING IN THE VILLAGE FOR A WHILE, SINBAD NOTICED A STRANGE SIGHT—MEN WITH WINGS!

NEVER HAD HE SEEN SUCH A THING.

THE NEXT TIME YOU FLY, TAKE ME WITH YOU.

ALL RIGHT ..., BUT YOU'LL HAVE TO BE CAREFUL.

PRAISE ALLAH!

IN HIS JOY AND AWE, SINBAD THANKED ALLAH FOR THE WONDERFUL FLIGHT.

AUUGHH!?

BUT HE SOON DISCOVERED THAT HE'D SPOKEN SOME DANGEROUS WORDS.

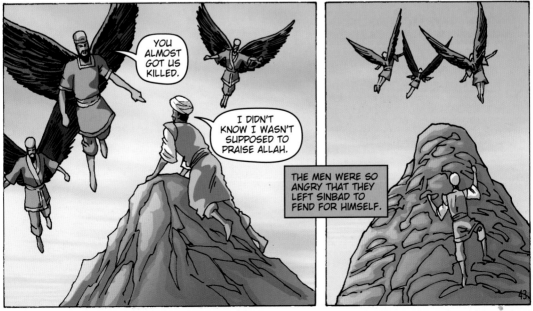

YOU ALMOST GOT US KILLED.

I DIDN'T KNOW I WASN'T SUPPOSED TO PRAISE ALLAH.

THE MEN WERE SO ANGRY THAT THEY LEFT SINBAD TO FEND FOR HIMSELF.

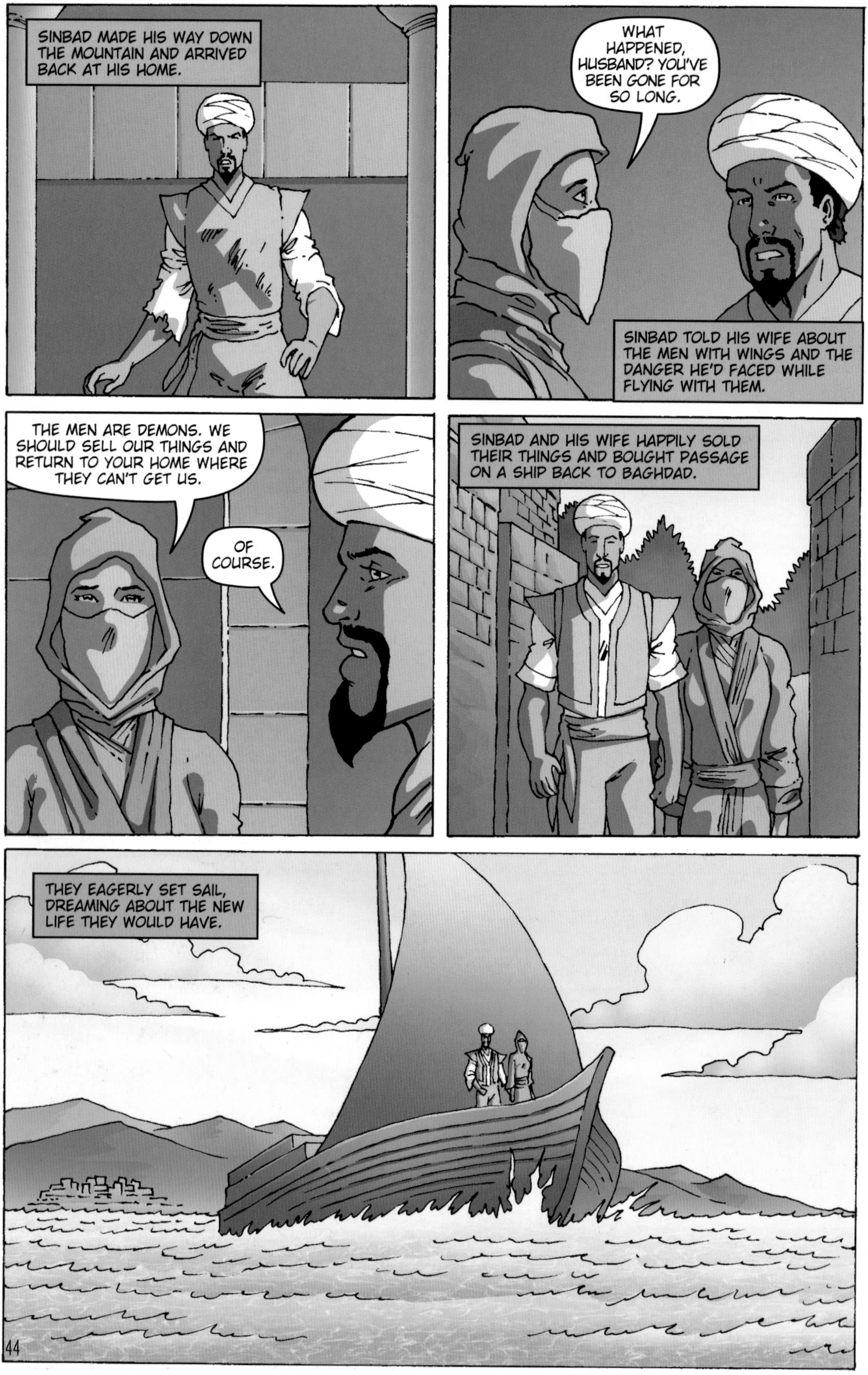
SINBAD MADE HIS WAY DOWN THE MOUNTAIN AND ARRIVED BACK AT HIS HOME.
WHAT HAPPENED, HUSBAND? YOU'VE BEEN GONE FOR SO LONG.
SINBAD TOLD HIS WIFE ABOUT THE MEN WITH WINGS AND THE DANGER HE'D FACED WHILE FLYING WITH THEM.
THE MEN ARE DEMONS. WE SHOULD SELL OUR THINGS AND RETURN TO YOUR HOME WHERE THEY CAN'T GET US.
OF COURSE.
SINBAD AND HIS WIFE HAPPILY SOLD THEIR THINGS AND BOUGHT PASSAGE ON A SHIP BACK TO BAGHDAD.
THEY EAGERLY SET SAIL, DREAMING ABOUT THE NEW LIFE THEY WOULD HAVE.

FRIENDS, I PRAISE ALLAH FOR ALL THE FORTUNE HE HAS GIVEN ME!

SINBAD KEPT HIS PROMISE TO NEVER AGAIN TRAVEL BY SEA.

HE AND HIS WIFE LIVED HAPPILY IN BAGHDAD FOR THE REST OF THEIR LIVES.

DO YOU HAVE ANOTHER STORY, DEAR WIFE?

OF COURSE, HUSBAND. THERE ARE HUNDREDS MORE STORIES TO TELL ...

GLOSSARY AND PRONUNCIATION GUIDE

ALLAH: the name for God in the Islamic faith

BAGHDAD: a city in the Middle Eastern country of Iraq. Baghdad is the country's capital.

BASSORAH (bah-*sohr*-ah): a city and port in the Middle Eastern country of Iraq. In modern times, Bassorah is called Basra.

CALIPH (*kahl*-if): a ruler in an Islamic community

FERMENT: to go through a chemical change. Fermentation is used to make different kinds of food and drinks.

GEM: a valuable stone

GOURD: a fruit with a round shape. Gourds are similar to pumpkins and squash.

MERCHANT: someone who makes money by selling goods

OGRE (*oh*-gur): a fierce monster

PORT: a place where boats and ships dock

REEF: a strip of coral, rock, or sand near the surface of a body of water

RUKH (*ruhk*): a mythical bird of great size and strength. Rukhs are said to live near the Indian Ocean.

SCHEHERAZADE (shuh-*hehr*-uh-zahd): the narrator of the *Arabian Nights* tales. She tells stories to her husband, the sultan, to win his favor and prove her worth.

SHEIKH (*shayk*): the leader of an Arab tribe or village

SULTAN: a king in some Muslim countries

TURBAN: a head covering made by winding a scarf around the head

FURTHER READING AND WEBSITES

Downing, David. *The Making of the Middle East*. Chicago: Raintree, 2006. Learn about the Middle East—the region of the world where the *Arabian Nights* began.

Fletcher, Susan. *Shadow Spinner*. New York: Aladdin Paperbacks, 1998. In this novel, a girl named Marjan saves Scheherazade from the sultan when the storyteller runs out of tales.

Leeson, Robert. *My Sister Shahrazad: Tales from the Arabian Nights*. London: Frances Lincoln, 2001. This volume includes stories such as *The Fisherman and the Jinni* and *The Dream*.

Smith, Philip. *Aladdin and Other Favorite Arabian Nights Stories*. Mineola, NY: Dover Publications, Inc., 1993. Read more *Arabian Nights* stories, including *Aladdin and the Wonderful Lamp*, *Ali Baba and the Forty Thieves*, and *The Enchanted Horse*.

Global Connections: The Middle East
http://www.pbs.org/wgbh/globalconnections/mideast/index.html
On this website, you'll find a timeline of Middle Eastern history as well as interesting information on the region's people and culture.

CREATING *SINBAD: SAILING INTO PERIL*

In creating this story, author Marie P. Croall worked from *Arabian Nights Volume I: The Marvels and Wonders of the Thousand and One Nights*, adapted from Richard F. Burton's unexpurgated translation by Jack Zipes. Artist Clint Hilinski worked in consultation with art historian Allan T. Kohl and used historical sources to shape the visual content of the tale. Together the text and artwork tell the story of Sinbad, a man who encountered many adventures and hardships in his travels on the high seas.

original pencil sketch from page 18

INDEX

ABOUT THE AUTHOR AND THE ARTIST

MARIE P. CROALL lives in Cary, North Carolina, with her loving husband and four wonderful cats. She has written for Marvel, DC Comics, Moonstone Books, Devils Due, and Harris Comics. She has also completed a self-published graphic novel and a short film. Croall has spent much of her life reading fables and legends from the Middle East and Asia and enjoys discovering new things about different cultures.

CLINT HILINSKI grew up in Esko, Minnesota, where he became interested in art at an early age. He continued studying art at the University of Wisconsin-Superior, where he received his bachelor's degree in fine art. Hilinski's influences include Jim Lee, Alan Davis, and Adam Hughes. He has worked as an illustrator for DC Comics, Image, Dark Horse, and many other companies. Hilinski has worked on titles such as *Justice League of America*, *Xena*, *Voltron*, and *GI Joe*.